Lions, Tigers, and Bears

Lions, Tigers, and Bears

Why Are Big Predators So Rare?

Ron Hirschi

Photographs by
Thomas D. Mangelsen

BOYDS MILLS PRESS

HONESDALE, PENNSYLVANIA

Text copyright © 2007 by Ron Hirschi
Photographs copyright © 2007 by Thomas D. Mangelsen

Boyds Mills Press, Inc.
815 Church Street
Honesdale, Pennsylvania 18431
Printed in China

Library of Congress Cataloging-in-Publication Data

Hirschi, Ron.
  Lions, tigers, and bears : why are big predators so rare? / Ron Hirschi ;
photographs by Thomas D. Mangelsen.—1st ed.
      p. cm.
  Includes bibliographical references and index.
  ISBN 978-1-59078-435-8 (hardcover : alk. paper)
  1. Predatory animals—Juvenile literature. 2. Wildlife conservation—Juvenile
literature. I. Mangelsen, Thomas D. II. Title.

QL758.H57 2007
591.5'3—dc22

                                    2006037956

First edition, 2007
The text of this book is set in 13-point Sabon.

10 9 8 7 6 5 4 3 2 1

CONTENTS

INTRODUCTION

I GREW UP AT THE EDGE OF the sea in the 1950s and 1960s. At that time, most people still believed the ocean was so vast that human activities couldn't affect its waters. Rivers flowing near my home held abundant runs of fish that, in turn, became healthy prey for large predators, including killer whales, which swam past me in my small boat. Dense, old forests grew nearby, and cougars wandered to the edge of our backyard. I was in awe of these creatures then. I am concerned about them now.

Today, the fish in the river are far fewer in number, and killer whales are endangered from pollution in my local waters. Forests don't tower as high and are not as widespread. These changes to the land and sea have harmed cougar and killer whale populations near my home. In more distant lands, fierce creatures like lions, tigers, and bears vanish for many of the same reasons. Scientists are working to find ways to protect habitat and remaining populations of big predators.

One hopeful sign for the future can be found in the return of our nation's symbol, the bald eagle. Like cougars, they had disappeared near my home when I was young. Their nesting trees had been cut down. They were even shot from the skies. Many more died from chemicals, especially one known as DDT, which was used to kill insects. When it entered the food chain, DDT caused the deaths of many birds, including eagles.

When I was in sixth grade, one powerful tool helped to eventually end the use of DDT and to protect many birds from vanishing. That tool was a pen used by one woman, Rachel Carson. Ms. Carson had observed the birds disappearing. She then turned her concern into words and wrote a book called *Silent Spring*. Her words warned of the dangers of DDT, and soon people rallied to stop its use. Today, bald eagles have returned, and I can say with much joy that no day goes by that my family and I don't see a bald eagle near our home. One concerned woman and one book were all that was needed to make the difference.

In the pages ahead, we will explore the world of the biggest, fiercest, and some of the rarest animals on earth. Maybe we will discover some ways we can all work together to help them survive into the future.

COUGAR

THE AIR IS HOT AND DRY.
The wind is still. A deer slumbers in the shade of tall pines where a chipmunk scurries from the lowest branches to perch atop a lichen-covered rock. Suddenly, without breaking the silence, a cougar leaps into view. Chipmunk and deer both scramble, trying to avoid this large American cat.

Seldom seen by humans, cougars are one of the most threatened large mammals of North America. Much of the threat comes when people move into former wild lands in the West to build second, third, and even fourth homes in the middle of cougar country. Deer survive in the midst of humans. Chipmunks do, too. For many reasons, cougars do not.

Also known as mountain lion, puma, and panther, the cougar is a solitary hunter. Unlike African lions, cougars shy away from their own kind for much of the year. Male cougars also wander widely, often roaming twenty miles or more in just one night. So they need large tracts of wild lands in order to thrive. Males and females travel together for a short time during breeding season.

Female cougars might give birth to anywhere from one to as many as six cubs. Once the cubs are born, females are protective mothers. They keep the cubs with them for one to two years and raise them on their own. Even in good habitat, only one or two cubs survive, since a mother cougar must have plentiful deer and other prey to raise her young with success.

Cougars have already lost much of their former habitat in the United States and now live mostly in western mountains. New housing developments continue to shrink this rugged region that once offered these animals a refuge. This is especially true where houses are built in rugged areas that were used only for hunting, fishing, and other temporary activities. Loss of habitat has also been severe in places like the Colorado River. Dams have flooded many miles of valuable riverbank habitat that in the past offered the cats excellent hunting and sheltered places to raise their young.

Riverbank, or riparian, habitat is a lush mixture of cottonwoods, willows, and other plants that don't mind, or even need, getting their roots wet. Where beavers dam a stream, riparian habitat expands to create even more of this lush living space that supports many birds and mammals. Beaver dams are low. Over time, they flood, then fill with new plant growth as beaver populations come and go. Not so human-made dams. Once in place, these dams flood with deep water. Over the years, they have destroyed thousands of miles of riparian habitat in our country. The cougar is but one creature to suffer from our actions.

Riparian habitat loss, forest clearing, and housing developments that roll across foothills into the cougar's home are all major causes of cougar

decline. Needing room to roam, the cougars of America need much help to survive into the future. That protection will be difficult as more and more people move into the last strongholds of the cougar.

Habitat loss doesn't usually happen overnight, but some forms of loss are quick to take shape. Our ability to live in and change mountainous areas is an example. Once, most people needed to live near

Cougars require safe shelters in their habitat.

cities for their jobs. Most others lived on farms at low elevations where soil is almost always deeper and richer than mountain soils. Human population in the mountains has always been somewhat low in large part because people were unable to grow crops.

Today, there is no need to grow our own food because of the ease of shipping goods from coast to

coast and from lowlands to mountaintop. More and more people can also live great distances from their jobs since computers allow them to telecommute from their homes. Modern four-wheel-drive vehicles have also made it easy to travel up steep, snowy mountain roads. These and other changes have now placed many people, their pets, and their homes in the middle of cougar country.

Mountain communities in Montana, Wyoming, Idaho, Colorado, and California are growing rapidly, owing in part to these new settlers and their technology-based jobs. Where cougars were once free to roam in search of deer and other prey, sprawling homesites now limit the big cat's ability to stalk its prey, raise its young, and, as a result, survive.

People living in mountainous regions are showing signs of concern and are rallying to educate others who live in or visit cougar country. Their efforts are aimed to help protect humans and the health of cougar populations. Simple actions such as making sure pets and livestock are protected within shelters and fences can reduce conflicts between cougars and domestic animals. Those who know the cats well also suggest that if you encounter a cougar in the wild, shout at the cat, make yourself look big, and even throw objects in its direction. Cougars generally avoid people, and these actions can prevent a potentially harmful experience.

POLAR BEAR

A MOTHER POLAR BEAR paddles through icy water with her cubs trailing behind. The mother bear is strong and well adapted to the water. She might even be able to swim across bodies of water fifty miles wide. Her cubs are not yet strong enough to keep up the pace, even on a much shorter swim. If they do tire, the little ones climb atop their mother's back for a welcome ride to the distant shore.

The polar bear has powerful front legs with large paws that help it to swim. The bear's great strength helps it to crush ice dens and snatch seals that hide beneath frozen shelters. Polar bears also feed on walrus, berries, and the carcasses of whales washed onto the shore.

Dead whales offer a tremendous feast often shared by several bears that are attracted to the odor of the carcass from many miles away. At these times of plenty, many polar bears will dine together with little or no conflict. When they meet, bears hug in dancing embraces and might roam together for many months. But the bears often live solitary lives in their Arctic home.

More than half of the world's polar bears live in Canada, but they are also present in the Arctic Circle, a vast area that covers one-sixth of the earth's

(right) On long water crossings, polar bear cubs will hitch a ride on their mother's back.

surface. This is a land of ice and snow with few people. The human population of New York City alone is more than twice that of the entire Arctic. But it is this human population far to the south of the polar bear's natural home that threatens the animal's future.

Unlike most threatened predators, polar bears are not in great danger from humans living nearby or moving into their natural landscapes. True, polar bears are shot by hunters, and bears do face problems in areas where they come into contact with human settlements. But the polar bear's habitat is now changing rapidly because of human activities in the world where most of us live, far to the south of the Arctic. Much of that threat comes from global warming.

Global warming occurs as carbon dioxide and other gases rise into the atmosphere. Warm rays that originate from the sun bounce off the earth and bounce back after bumping into this layer of gases. This is known as the greenhouse effect since the gas layer acts like the glass that traps warmth from the sun within a gardener's greenhouse.

Climate reports show that much of the impact of this warming is most pronounced in the polar north. Scientists have observed a 7 percent reduction in the Arctic's ice cover in only twenty-five years. Ice is also becoming much thinner.

In many ways, the ice is critical for the polar bear's survival. Seals are the polar bear's most important prey in much of the bear's range. They hunt seals on the ice and need a solid, frozen layer

to reach their prey. When the ice melts, they are like hockey players without a rink and have no way to reach their goal. Bears in western Hudson Bay have shown lower reproduction rates as spring thaws cause ice to melt earlier than in times past. Scientists have also expressed concern that decreased ice cover also means wider and wider reaches between landmasses. Polar bears are excellent swimmers, but cubs and young bears will have increasing difficulty reaching land. Those with a mother to help them may survive, but even the strongest swimmers may not be able to cover the distances created as ice continues to vanish.

Scientists believe that polar bears are a signal to all of us. Prior to scientific observations that called attention to global warming, polar bear populations were thought to be stable, even increasing. Most books published as recently as the 1990s made no mention of serious threats to their numbers. In fact, polar bears benefited from international agreements that protected them throughout their range. Now, most scientists agree that the polar bear is threatened. As its icy world changes, we all suffer its losses and with that loss comes an early warning of changes to our more immediate world.

Scientists have voiced concern by recommending that the U.S. government place the polar bear on

Polar bears can grow more than seven feet tall and weigh more than seventeen hundred pounds.

the endangered species list. This would be the first time an animal was considered for protection under our endangered species laws as a result of global warming. If the bears are listed as an endangered species with the United States Fish and Wildlife Service (USFWS), scientists will have greater abilities to turn ideas into actions that could lead to the polar bear's protection.

This same kind of legal protection took place when bald eagles were in danger of extinction. They were listed under the provisions of the Endangered Species Act and protected according to the rules used by the USFWS. Like many legal actions, this took a great deal of time. But in the end, protective measures to save habitat and remove threats saved the bald eagle. Polar bears can become a success story as well.

Polar bears gather where food is abundant. Melting ice, however, threatens their hunting grounds.

LION

A FEMALE LION SLOWLY stalks her prey through grasses as golden as her sleek fur. The lioness is skilled in the chase, and she is often joined by other females as they sniff the air, listen intently, and watch one another like team members in a soccer match. Moving closer and closer, the lion suddenly bursts from her crawl to run down a zebra, wildebeest, or gazelle. Females hunt together in the chase. They also raise their young together in a pride, the lion's extended family unit.

Without doubt, the lion is the most recognizable member of the cat family. The lion's roar greets theatergoers at the beginning of certain movies, and most nature programs set in Africa include images of lions. Lions were once widespread, living through-out the world, even in North and South America. They disappeared from Europe about two thousand years ago. Over the past two hundred years, lions have also disappeared from the Middle East and northern Africa.

Today, lions continue to vanish from their dwindling homelands in Africa, where they survive mainly in parks and other lands managed to protect wildlife. A small population of lions also exists in India. Like tigers, people see lions mostly in zoos, where they are bred successfully to maintain captive populations around the world.

Lions in the wild are majestic creatures that once attracted big game safari hunters determined to bring home a lion pelt. Now lions attract tourists who visit Africa to bring home photographs of sleek females hunting or stately males resting in the shade. While females typically live within the pride with related females, males are often solitary and nomadic, wandering widely. These nomads are mainly young males who will eventually challenge other males in fierce battle to take over a pride.

Two or three males, often brothers, defend the pride. Their roar lets other lions know they are present, and their urine markings help to define the pride's boundaries. But a fight to the death often determines the new male within a pride. These pride males father all the young and take the first and most food when females return with prey. When we say someone gets the "lion's share" of a meal, we really mean the "male lion's share."

A day in the life of the lion pride seems like a lazy slumber filled with occasional fights and lots of friendly touching, licking, and purring. A lioness gives birth to two or three cubs, often at the same time as other females within the pride. As night falls, females typically slink away, leaving their young in the care of sisters, aunts, or grandmothers. The pressure to capture more prey increases as new cubs are born, and females have better success when hunting at night.

Teamwork within the pride helps to ensure survival of each member. Young ones left in the care of adults are protected from predators, including other lions that are not members of the pride. But the pride and surrounding nomadic males must find food within an African landscape that is rapidly changing.

Lions live within parks, where their protection is fairly secure. Like grizzly bears in and around Yellowstone National Park, African lions do not recognize park boundaries. There are no fences holding them inside these safe areas, so lions often wander beyond the refuges.

Many lions living outside park boundaries are threatened by increased habitat loss as land is cleared and developed for farming. Lions are shot when they prey on livestock. Their habitat is also undergoing fragmentation at a rapid rate. This means that each space they need as a home shrinks in size as human settlements expand. It also means that greater distances now exist between suitable habitats. As each of their living areas grows smaller, lions are unable to move to a new habitat that may be many miles away.

Like most large predators, lions need a great deal of human understanding if they are to survive. People who live in lion country may come to realize how they can profit through tourism, as visitors come in search of the prides with cameras, not guns. As long as people value wild lions in wild landscapes, we will all enjoy the sight of these majestic creatures.

CHEETAH

A FEMALE CHEETAH AND her three cubs rest atop a termite mound as if they were mountain climbers resting after reaching the summit of an ancient mountaintop. Look closely at the faces of these swift cats and you will first notice what appear to be tear stains. Dark lines trace from their eyes to outline their nose.

Spots help to camouflage the cheetah, and its eye lines may prevent prey from noticing that the cheetah is watching, waiting, and ready to pounce. Like most predators, the cheetah has keen eyesight. They can see the slightest movement in the surrounding grassland, and the female atop her termite hill soon slips down from her perch to catch a meal for her young ones.

No one, not even the fastest Olympic athlete, could ever match the running ability of a cheetah. Built to chase down swift gazelles and other herding animals, the cheetah is sleek and strong and has been clocked at more than seventy miles per hour in short bursts. Spots and coloration help blend the cheetah into the dry grasses of the African savannah, where scattered trees supply shade and broad grasslands offer hunting grounds.

Cheetahs survive where prey is abundant and habitat is protected.

Unlike the lion, cheetahs hunt alone. Humans have long regarded the cheetah with great reverence, even training the cats to hunt. Asian royalty once tamed cheetahs, wrapped them in elegant robes to keep them warm, and placed leather hoods over their heads as blindfolds, which calmed the swift hunters prior to the chase. Over the past several hundred years, humans have reduced the animal's natural habitat and killed off gazelles and other prey, leading to a slow but steady decline in the cheetah population.

Once found in India, the Middle East, and most of Africa, the cheetah is now gone from much of its former range. But cheetahs hang on in perilously small numbers. They live in places that may surprise those who think cheetahs exist only in a land of blistering sun and dry grasses.

A group of young Iranian scientists has recently created an organization to help protect the cheetah population in their country. Fifty or fewer cheetahs are thought to survive in Iran, preying on wild sheep and goats and other mammals in a rocky landscape where snow covers the ground in winter. Cheetahs in the snow may not reflect the typical image of these spotted cats, but the Iranian cheetahs have found a way to survive in that country, and possibly in neighboring Afghanistan and Pakistan.

Greater numbers survive in southern Africa where the cheetah is fairly abundant in Namibia. Here, too, habitat loss and natural threats pose dangers to the cheetah population. Cheetahs are preyed upon by leopards, lions, and hyenas. Swift, but not as strong, cheetahs suffer when competing with these other predators. Cheetah cubs are especially vulnerable.

Cheetahs also suffer at the hands of poachers and wildlife dealers who sell live cheetahs as well as pelts, both legally and illegally. Farmers and ranchers also kill cheetahs in response to livestock losses. But some creative livestock management procedures are working. Ranchers in many areas are encouraged to use guard dogs to protect their livestock, a practice that has already shown reductions in cheetah deaths.

Like other large predators, the cheetah has suffered from loss of habitat. It can run with the greatest speed of any land animal, but it cannot run away from bulldozers and sprawling civilization. If people fail to practice tolerance and preserve the animal's protective refuges, the cheetah will continue to vanish.

Cheetah survival in the Middle East may also be threatened by wars and the threats of wars. Hostilities in the region prevent scientists from putting in place much needed environmental protection for the cheetahs. Funds and human resources also are lost when billions of dollars are spent on tanks, bombs, and other weapons. Imagine a world in which we fought against the causes of environmental destruction instead of going to war. Maybe then, people would rally together to work for peace while saving cheetahs.

TIGER

WHEN SPORTS TEAMS CHOOSE a mascot, they usually pick an animal with great strength and powers beyond our own. Detroit, Michigan, chose the tiger for its Major League Baseball team. So have hundreds of schools. The tiger's face appears in many other places, and the animal's great growl is a well-known signal that it is time to eat breakfast. To find real, wild tigers, search the deep forests of India, where they continue to prowl.

The truth is that more tigers live in captivity today than in their natural habitats. Normally solitary, tigers are dangerous predators. Like tiger sharks, they will attack people, making it difficult to maintain tiger-friendly neighborhoods in some regions of the world. It is one thing to visit a zoo and watch a tiger that lives behind steel bars. It is another to reside in a village within a forest where tigers may make you or your brothers and sisters their next meal. Unlike cougars, tigers are not easily frightened, making it all the more difficult to live in their midst.

Tigers are the largest of the world's cats, but they vary in size within their wide range. Smaller subspecies of tigers inhabit or recently disappeared from scattered parts of India and southeastern Asia. The largest subspecies, the Siberian tiger, still lives in northeastern Asia. Siberian tigers may weigh up to five hundred pounds and can devour as much as one hundred pounds in a single meal.

Unmistakable with their striking orange coats striped with black, the tiger is perfectly camouflaged in tall grasses and dark forests. Their coats are somewhat lighter in color in the north, where the Siberian tiger often hunts in forests and open, mountainous areas covered in snow.

Like grizzly bears in the early days of settlement in the western United States, the number of tigers declined in Asia because people feared them and killed them. Habitat loss is now a greater threat to their populations, but there is new hope for tigers' survival in their northernmost homelands.

Small numbers of Siberian tigers still live in North Korea and China and roam a vast forested region of eastern Russia where the human population is low. This forest is of great value to the Russian people, and the changing economy in that country has sparked new interests in logging trees within tiger territories.

Scientists have been working to protect tigers in these forests, where population counts in 1996 estimated the total population at about 370 tigers. The 2004 tiger census involved many concerned people, who estimated an increase to about 400 tigers. This is a fairly large fraction of the world's wild tiger population, which is thought to number from about 3,500 to as many as 5,000.

Turning their attention from tiger counts, scientists are now working with loggers to encourage tiger-friendly forests. In many cases, they are winning this struggle in Russian woodlands, where enormous old-growth trees are very valuable. Like rain forests, these Siberian woodlands provide homes for many other animals. So far, tiger protectors have gained success in convincing loggers to thin the forests rather than clearcut, meaning cutting down all the trees in a given area.

But scientists continue to worry about road building, which is necessary to transport the trees out of the forest. This same problem threatens forest animals throughout the world and poses a real threat to tigers. Siberian tigers live in mountainous forests where no roads have existed in the past. With the roads come more people. Some are poachers who use these new pathways to hunt tigers illegally. Poaching is now the leading cause of death of Siberian tigers.

Increasing threats from poachers pose an even greater danger to tigers in India, once thought to be the last best stronghold for the striped cats. Indian tiger populations have declined from about 4,500 in the 1980s to as low as 2,000 or fewer in 2006. In some regions of the world, tiger parts are used as ingredients in certain medicines that are very expensive. The high prices encourage illegal poaching. The demand for tiger parts is especially great in China, South Korea, and the United States.

Preserves have long been a safety zone for tigers and other large predators. But Indian, or Bengal, tigers are now threatened in many of these former sanctuaries. According to the World Wildlife Fund, some of these preserves have already lost their entire population of tigers. The decline has motivated United Nations officials to call for greater protection, but with increasing value placed on tiger parts, it is difficult to control poaching.

A hopeful sign comes from the prime minister of India, who is encouraging greater protection. Another ray of hope for the tiger comes from Japan. As the country did in the past to protect elephants from ivory hunters, Japan has placed bans on tiger imports. Educational efforts are also helping to stop the illegal imports that still take place in China. If the Chinese are able to prevent this activity, poachers will have no market for their tiger kills. That is a strong hope for the tiger's future.

And yet, a larger threat may be right at our doorstep. According to the World Wildlife Fund, the United States is the second-largest illegal importer of tiger parts. We need to protect our borders from the same unethical and highly illegal importation of tiger parts if it is not too late.

GRIZZLY BEAR

A COOL WIND RUSTLES the leaves along the Yellowstone River in Yellowstone National Park, Wyoming. It is spring, and mountain wildflowers poke through the edges of melting snow here in the high country. A small herd of elk grazes near a patch of pine trees not far from the rushing river.

Large boulders are scattered in the clearings between the trees, most with bright-colored patches of lichens that look like paintings left by visiting artists. But one of the rocks is slightly darker. It begins to move, and the elk sense it isn't a rock at all. With a burst of speed to match any racehorse, the "rock" suddenly runs straight toward one of the younger elk. Like a football linebacker bringing down a running back, the predator, a grizzly bear, tackles and wins this match.

Grizzly bears are immense and strong. They can weigh more than a thousand pounds and prey on large animals, including elk, deer, and even moose. Similar to other bears, they are omnivorous and feed on a wide range of plants, berries, insects, and fish in addition to larger quarry. In Alaska, the grizzly is known as a brown bear and feeds on salmon. Alaskan brown bears often gather in large numbers to grasp the slippery fish in pools, riffles, and at

falls where the salmon hesitate before leaping. Sometimes the leap is interrupted by a huge, gaping mouth lined with sharp teeth.

Brown bears also live in eastern Russia, where they come together for a salmon feast just as they do in Alaska. But the Russian bears gather in far greater numbers. In fact, Russia supports the largest numbers of grizzly (brown) bears in the world.

Although Russian bear populations are high, threats to their existence are similar to those that North American grizzlies faced in the past. Habitat loss, overhunting, and human encroachment all threaten the bears. Like North Americans in the early 1800s, Russians probably find it difficult to comprehend this threat because their forests are so vast and prey is still abundant.

The Taiga, an area of about 1.5 million square miles, covers nearly one-fourth of Russia. This vast land is mostly forest, with little or no human settlements to disturb native fish and wildlife. The same could have been said of much of the western United States when the grizzly bear lived in harmony with other native wildlife in California, Oregon, Colorado, and other states where it has vanished.

Similar to Siberian tigers, the Russian brown bear is hunted, and the increase in the number of kills is a serious concern to bear biologists. A growing hope is that Russian biologists will be able to protect bear habitat and control hunting before bear populations decline as severely as they did in the United States during the past century.

North American grizzly bear populations have been protected in many ways, such as through the Endangered Species Act. This is the same protection

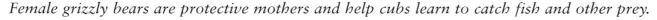

Female grizzly bears are protective mothers and help cubs learn to catch fish and other prey.

under consideration for polar bears. The U.S. Fish and Wildlife Service has set strict guidelines for deciding where and when a bear population needs protection from human activities, which includes a ban on hunting. Now, however, the USFWS may remove grizzlies around Yellowstone National Park from its special listing as an endangered species. This raises concerns for many people who believe the bears deserve more time to roam away from the park and establish populations in former habitat without threats from hunting. Others argue that the grizzly bear can be managed like other wildlife, allowing hunting seasons to control their numbers. Some also believe the bear has no place in the wild that now includes homes as well as ranches for cattle and sheep.

In 1975 the total grizzly population in and near Yellowstone was approximately two hundred. Today there are about six hundred. Scientists believe this number can and will increase by about 4 percent each year, given current conditions. The USFWS and bear biologists should be commended for helping the bears increase in numbers, but threats to their habitat appear to be rising at a rate that is greater than the rate of their protective measures. Suburban sprawl stretches up and down the valleys of Montana and Wyoming as new residents, attracted by the beauty of the region as well as the abundance of fish and wildlife, move into the greater Yellowstone area. The bears cannot compete with an expanding population that brings with it new homes and shopping centers.

Small signs of hope remain despite the growth of human settlement in the West. Groups of people have joined together to form land trusts, purchasing lands for the bears. These groups also buy the "rights to develop" from landowners. This means that a person gives up his or her right to build homes or other structures on multiple acres in exchange for payment. These development rights help create vast tracts of land used by elk to over-winter, by moose to browse, and by grizzly bears to roam free in search of a meal and a safe place to build a winter den. More and more people see protection of remaining wilderness lands as a positive way to protect the grizzly and its mountain habitats. Making sure the grizzly remains a thriving part of the mountain woodlands is just as important to many westerners as keeping the Red Sox in Boston, the Liberty Bell in Philadelphia, or the Statue of Liberty in New York's harbor.

Grizzly bears dine on fish in Alaska and in Rocky Mountain rivers and streams.

KILLER WHALE

A FERRY FILLED WITH commuters, shoppers, and tourists pulls away from the busy Seattle waterfront into Elliott Bay in western Washington State. A short distance from the dock, the ferry intercom clicks on and the captain announces that a pod of killer whales is swimming just off the starboard side of the boat. Passengers hurry to the windows and deck railings to watch the sleek whales as they dive and leap in the steel blue waters of Puget Sound.

The killer whales, also known as orcas, slice through the waves, well in view of the ferry passengers and anyone walking along the busy downtown waterfront of this West Coast seaport. One of the whales dives right at the bow of the boat, surfacing with a meal. It has captured a seal and thrashes its prey on the surface of the water.

Unseen by human eyes, the seal had been feasting earlier in the day, dining on lingcod that had moved into shallow waters to lay eggs along rocky shores. The lingcod had eaten a rock cod that had eaten a flounder, one of the more numerous fish in Elliott Bay. A butter clam had been the flounder's last meal.

(right) Scientists can identify individual killer whales from their body markings and dorsal-fin size and shape.

From butter clam to flounder and up the food chain to killer whale, this web of marine life has thrived in our oceans for many centuries. The whales have fed on fish, seals, and other whales with little interference from humans—that is, until recently.

Unlike the grizzly bear or tiger, killer whales are not threatened by humans. A few have been captured for theme parks. Cargo ships and other traffic on the seas disturb their lives. Humans, for the most part, don't settle in large numbers within killer whale habitat, and the animals are not hunted for food or sport. But civilization is harming the whales in far more unsettling ways.

Unseen by most people, chemicals wash into the sea from our homes, shops, and factories. Some of these chemicals may be found only in small amounts in certain animals, but they become more concentrated in the bodies of others as they move through food chains. Certain chemicals become a serious problem for killer whales when the chemicals reach high levels through bioaccumulation.

Bioaccumulation means that chemicals increase, or accumulate, within an animal's body for biological reasons that are often unique to that creature. In Washington State, bioaccumulation has been observed in killer whales when chemicals known as PCBs (polychlorinated biphenyls) build up in the animal's fatty tissues.

PCBs are so harmful to life in general that they have been banned for use in the United States. They are still used in some countries for many industrial purposes and continue to be disposed of throughout the world. They make their way into ocean food webs as industrial waste is burned and drops from the sky. PCBs also flow into the sea in chemical spills in and around cities.

PCBs may enter the whale's food chain in low levels, but they dissolve readily in fat. As a seal feeds, any PCB that enters its body dissolves in the layer of fat beneath the skin. Over time, the amount of PCBs within seal blubber increases to a level that can cause reproductive failures, deformities, and other problems for the seal.

When killer whales feed on seals that have PCBs within their fatty tissues, the chemicals begin to accumulate in the whale's thick layer of blubber. PCBs and other chemicals that bioaccumulate also increase within the rich, fatty milk of female killer whales.

Because PCBs and similar chemicals build up in its mother's milk, a newborn killer whale may be nourished with liquid that is harmful to its development. At the same time, a nursing mother "gets rid of" a lot of her harmful chemical load while feeding her calf. Since males produce no milk, they have no way of losing their toxic chemicals, and scientists typically find that males have twice the levels of toxins as females their age.

Among the other chemicals that threaten killer whales are those used in fire-resistant treatment of carpets, car parts, and other products used in homes and industry.

In the recent past, high concentrations of PCBs were found in fish, seals, and killer whales. Now scientists fear that a new chemical used for much the same purposes as PCBs is threatening the whales in many ways. The levels of PBDEs, or polybrominated diphenyl ethers, are increasing in ocean environments, and Canadian biologists warn that the presence of these chemicals in killer whales may likely alter the animal's brain development. Once they enter food chains, both PCBs and PBDEs last for many years. The combination of the two within the whales may affect the mammal's reproduction, leading to severe losses in population. The chemicals are also thought to damage the immune systems of whales, weakening their ability to fight disease.

Visitors to Puget Sound admire the beauty of the sea, splendor of the mountains, and the fresh air drifting in from the ocean. It is almost impossible to imagine how whales could be in any danger in such a spectacular corner of the Pacific Northwest. It might be wise to realize how all life is connected and that most of our waterways do eventually wash into the sea. Waste from Seattle certainly enters marine food chains, but contaminating chemicals also reach the sea from far more distant locations.

Like polar bears in the Arctic, killer whales have become another example of how animals can be affected by distant threats. Since we eat many of the same sea creatures within the killer whale's food chain, we should also consider how these threats might affect our own lives. Scientists are now urging legislation to protect the whales and to ban the manufacture and use of PBDEs, as has been done in Europe. Scientists have already been successful in securing endangered species status for Puget Sound killer whales.

Scientists hope that protection under the Endangered Species Act will help generate more funding to protect the whale's habitat. This would include aid in controlling harmful chemicals from entering the ocean and providing more protection for whale prey species such as salmon, a valuable fish in the Pacific Northwest.

The killer whales swimming in Washington waters are well studied and loved by many people who hop aboard whale-watching boats to see the sea mammals up close. Biologists have identified individual whales by size, shape, and markings on their dorsal fins. They have also come to know social groups, called pods. These pods, somewhat like a pride of lions, are tightly knit groupings that call to one another as they feed, travel, and play.

Recent findings also show that killer whales may stay together for long periods of time in part

because they have evolved an ability to share with one another. A mother whale will chomp chunks of salmon, letting them drop to the waiting mouth of a young one. Young whales also share with others. This behavior is uncommon in the animal kingdom, but not unexpected among killer whales. They swim together, play together, and stay together. They will continue to live with us if we can find ways to keep their water healthy.

One way to protect their habitat is already making an impact. Kids in the greater Puget Sound area learn about whale habitats, then they take steps to protect beaches, streams, and other areas. Many kids participate in stream projects to restore endangered salmon runs. Others encourage parents to stop using harmful chemicals on their lawns, creating "Whale-Friendly Yards." Some are trying to protect kelp forests, a valuable habitat of seaweed that can grow up to one hundred feet in height from the sea floor. These majestic kelp forests create a rich feeding ground for many sea creatures. They are often frequented by killer whales that come to feast on fish hidden in the shelter of the forest.

Mysteriously, some kelp forests are disappearing. When they do, valuable habitat is lost. When the habitat vanishes, many other species also disappear, including dense schools of herring and other valuable forage fish that require kelp for their own survival. Using new techniques developed by kelp biologists, kids are learning ways to correct and even restore this loss of kelp habitat. Little by little, they may find a way to bring back the kelp that supports a healthy population of clams, rockfish, salmon, and seals that nourish a healthy population of whales.

HOW TO HELP LARGE PREDATORS

If you live in a city or any place distant from bears, lions, or whales, it is probably hard to imagine how you can help these large predators. But all things on our fragile planet are connected, and your actions, no matter how small, can help. Remember, too, that almost all rivers and streams within our country eventually flow to the sea. Your actions to protect water quality in the middle of the United States can help ensure that clean water enters the mouth of a whale.

If you recycle, you are taking another action that helps protect our waters while reducing waste on the planet. If you talk to friends and family about the needs of wildlife, you are helping, too. And if you make others aware of the problems facing lions, tigers, and bears, you help bring greater knowledge and understanding to people who just might make a big difference.

Join local environmental groups at your school and in your community to learn more about helping plants and wildlife as well as the larger world. The following organizations might also help spark ideas. They include some of the groups around the world that devote time to helping large cats, whales, and bears. Take a look at their Web sites. Think about what you can do to help. Then take some action, big or small. You can be the person to think of a new idea that just might save an animal from extinction. Imagine that!

COUGAR
The Cougar Fund:
www.cougarfund.org

POLAR BEAR
Center for Biological Diversity:
www.biologicaldiversity.org

LION
World Wildlife Fund:
www.worldwildlife.org

CHEETAH
Iranian Cheetah Society:
www.iraniancheetah.org

TIGER
Save the Tiger Fund:
www.savethetigerfund.org

GRIZZLY BEAR
The Vital Ground Foundation:
www.vitalground.org
Greater Yellowstone Coalition:
www.greateryellowstone.org

KILLER WHALE
Whale and Dolphin Conservation Society:
www.wdcs.org
American Cetacean Society:
www.acsonline.org
American Cetacean Society, Puget Sound Chapter:
www.acspugetsound.org

INDEX